TRUE or FALSE?

These shoes are not just for tiptoeing around—they can also help a spy listen.

TRUE!

The KGB was the spy agency for the former Soviet Union—which used to be the United States' worst enemy. KGB agents would plant a tiny microphone and transmitter in the heel of a target's shoe. The agents could then listen in on the target's conversations.

Keep reading to find out about more spy gadgets.

Book design Red Herring Design/NYC

Library of Congress Cataloging-in-Publication Data
Rauf, Don, 1961—
Killer lipstick: and other spy gadgets / by Don Rauf.
p. cm.—(24/7: science behind the scenes)
Includes bibliographical references and index.
ISBN-13: 978-0-531-12084-2 (lib. bdg.) 978-0-531-17536-1 (pbk.)
ISBN-10: 0-531-12084-8 (lib. bdg.) 0-531-17536-7 (pbk.)
1. Espionage—Equipment and supplies—Juvenile literature. I. Title.
UB270.5.R38 2007
327.120028'4—dc22 2006021235

Published simultaneously in Canada. Printed in the United States of America.

KILLER LIPSTICK

And Other Spy Gadgets

Don Rauf

WARNING: This book could make you paranoid. You could start to imagine that your hall pass is a tracking device. Or that the clock on the wall is watching you. Or that the custodian is a spy . . .

Franklin Watts
An Imprint of Scholastic Inc.
New York • Toronto • London • Auckland • Sydney
Mexico City • New Delhi • Hong Kong
Danbury, Connecticut

CONTENTS

SPY 411

Before you snoop through the case files, check out this info.

Find out about the gadgets used during these real-life espionage missions.

Hitler's secret code was unbreakable. Or so he thought.

17

Case #1:
Breaking the Code

Hitler had crushed Europe and was taking aim at Britain. Could a group of brainy code breakers beat Germany's high-tech code machine?

27

Case #2:
A Secret Plan

After an anti-American leader took over in Cuba, the CIA tried to get rid of him—in some very strange ways.

The U.S. feared Cuban leader Fidel Castro.

This spy (on the left) made millions selling U.S. secrets.

37

Case #3:
An American Traitor

John Walker seemed like the guy next door. But for 17 years, he was the Soviet Union's most successful spy.

5

Pinkerton's National "WE NEVER SLEEP." Detective Agency

Know your enemy. That's the best military strategy. The more a country knows about its enemies, the safer it is.

SPY 411

That's where spies come in. They help gather that knowledge.

Some spies are secret agents who work overseas. They rely on informants who pass them tips. Others stay at home, supporting the agents in the field.

IN THIS SECTION:

▶ how spies really talk;

▶ believe-it-or-not spy gadgets and gizmos;

▶ and who else is part of the spy team.

Undercover Speak

Experts in espionage have their own way of speaking. Find out what their vocabulary means.

intelligence
(in-TEL-uh-juhnss)
information about an enemy's plans or activities

We've got to tail this guy and find out where he's getting his intelligence.

I don't like following people around in the rain. Maybe I should never have —*ahh-choo*! —gone into espionage.

espionage
(ESS-pee-uh-nahzh) using spies to gain information about the plans and activities of other groups, armies, or countries

Shh! And stop sneezing. He'll figure out he's under surveillance.

surveillance
(sur-VAY-luhnss) the act of keeping a close watch or listening in on somebody. It is often done in secret.

Say What?

The chief just texted me. But I can't figure out what code he used for the message.

code
(kode)
a system used to disguise a message by changing the words into something else. Letters, words, or phrases are replaced by other letters, words, phrases, or even symbols.

It's just a simple cipher code. All he did was replace A with B, B with C, and so on. His message says . . . *gezundheit*!

cipher
(SYE-fur)
a kind of code in which letters and numbers are replaced with other letters and numbers

Here's more spy lingo.

bug
(buhg) a hidden electronic listening device
*"We stuck a **bug** under the park bench so we could hear their conversation."*

handler
(HAN-dlur) a spy's boss
*"I'm waiting for instructions from my **handler**."*

mole
(mohl) a spy who works within the enemy's spy agency
*"They had a **mole** inside who told them our plans."*

rabbit
(RAB-it) the target of a surveillance operation
in the wind used to describe a target who escapes
*"The **rabbit** just got into a cab. He's **in the wind**."*

sleeper
(SLEE-puhr) an agent who isn't active and is living as a normal citizen in another country
*"She was a **sleeper** for five years before this mission."*

Killer Lipstick?

Spies have come up with some clever—and crazy—designs for their gadgets. Here's a look at some spy gadgets that aren't always exactly what they seem.

Killer Smile Some female **agents** in the **Soviet Union** used guns disguised as lipsticks. They were designed to fire a single shot at close range.

In the Money **CIA** agents hid messages and microfilm inside hollow silver dollars. Other coins had tiny radio transmitters planted inside them.

SPYCAMS
Cameras are one of a **spy**'s most important tools. They come in all shapes and sizes.

Flash Photography Japanese spies had lighters with cameras inside them. They could take somebody's photo while lighting a cigarette.

I'm Watching You A spy wearing a camera-watch could take pictures while pretending to check the time. This one's from Germany, but spies from many countries have used similar devices.

Pigeon Spies The CIA wanted to use pigeons to take pictures of enemy territory. In early tests, the cameras were so heavy the birds had to walk home. The CIA later developed much lighter cameras. Did the pigeons ever fly any successful **missions**? The CIA isn't saying.

11

THE NATURAL TOUCH
The strangest gadgets are those
designed to mimic animals,
insects, and other natural things.

A Fish Named Charlie The CIA has a 24-inch-long (61-cm-long) robotic catfish (*above*) that can swim among other fish. It can be sent anywhere in the world to spy on—who? Other catfish? Actually, it was probably designed to collect water samples near suspected nuclear or chemical plants. One problem is that it's so realistic that predators might try to eat it. The CIA won't say why they called it Charlie. That's classified information.

Stumped Commanders at a Soviet military base in the 1970s didn't know they were being spied on by a tree stump. The CIA had placed this fake stump in the woods near the base. It held a listening device that could record the base's secret radio messages. The stump then **transmitted** that information to a satellite, which sent it to the CIA.

Doo Drop In This gadget was a transmitter disguised as dog doo. An operative would leave it at a specific location, and it would transmit radio signals that guided aircraft to that spot. The CIA used it in the 1970s for reconnaissance missions or air strikes.

DELIVERING THE GOODS

Spies often need to pass secret documents to other agents without meeting in person. They do that by using **dead drops**. A dead drop involves hiding an item in an everyday object such as a trash bag. The spy leaves the object someplace where another agent can pick it up later.

A Traitor's Trash **FBI** agent Robert Phillip Hanssen sold thousands of U.S. military secrets to the Soviets. He would hide top-secret documents inside a garbage bag, which he left at an agreed-upon dead drop location. He would then pick up another garbage bag that the Soviets had left nearby. That one contained his payment. The bag in this photo was recovered by the FBI when they arrested Hanssen in 2001. They found $50,000 inside it.

Buried Treasure Some CIA agents use a special metal spike for dead drops. A spy puts film or other items inside a pointed tube and then shoves it into the ground. Since the spike is waterproof, it can even be placed in a shallow stream.

Techno-Rock In 2006, British agents in Russia were caught using a new kind of dead drop: a fake rock filled with high-tech electronics. They placed the rock on a busy city street. An **informant** could walk by and transmit data from a small digital device to the rock. Later, an agent could upload that information to his handheld computer.

13

The Spy Team

In the U.S., about 100,000 people work for the CIA and other intelligence agencies. They provide the government with information about threats to national security.

SPIES

These CIA agents work undercover to collect intelligence overseas. They work with contacts and sources that provide tips and information. Much of their work is focused on terrorism.

HANDLERS

Also known as spy masters, they oversee undercover agents to make sure they gather the kind of information that intelligence officials in Washington need. They often work undercover.

DIRECTOR OF NATIONAL INTELLIGENCE

This person is head of all the different intelligence agencies and advises the president about intelligence issues.

LANGUAGE OFFICERS

They support agents in the field as translators. They also provide information about other cultures.

ENGINEERS AND SCIENTISTS

The CIA depends on the latest cutting-edge technologies. Its scientists and engineers design and operate the systems and gadgets that allow agents to locate, track, and record people.

ANALYSTS

They take intelligence that comes in from all over the globe and figure out its importance and value. They report their findings to officials at all levels of government. Many focus on the plans of terrorist groups.

TRUE-LIFE CASE FILES!

24 hours a day, 7 days a week, 365 days a year, someone is spying on someone. And they're probably using a gadget or two to get the job done.

IN THIS SECTION:

▶ how a team of brainiacs tried to break a code—and save the world;

▶ the CIA's attempts to get rid of a Cuban leader;

▶ a traitor who sold U.S. secrets for 17 years.

Throughout history, people have sent each other secret messages. Here are some of the coding systems they used.

Belted Code

In fifth-century Sparta, soldiers wrapped a strip of leather along the length of a pole called a scytale. Then they wrote a message on it. When the strip was unwrapped, the letters made no sense. The receiver would have to wrap the strip around an identical pole to be able to read the message.

Butterfly Code

Robert Baden Powell (1857–1941) was the founder of the International Scouting Movement. As a spy in the late 19th century, he would pretend to be a butterfly collector. But his drawings of butterflies actually contained information about enemy forts. In this example, the outline of a fort is visible around the butterfly's body. Spots on the wing were code for the size and location of the fort's cannons.

Western Europe
1940-1944

Breaking the Code

Hitler had crushed most of Europe and
was taking aim at Britain. Could a group
of brainy code breakers beat
Germany's high-tech
code machine?

A Secret Weapon

German subs are sinking supply ships. Unless the subs are stopped, Britain will lose the war.

In 1940, World War II was raging across Europe. Nazi Germany had conquered most of Europe. Britain stood alone against the enemy. Adolf Hitler, the Nazi leader, planned to invade Britain next.

The British were barely managing to hold on. They desperately needed help. The United States had not officially entered the war. But it was definitely on Britain's side. To help its **ally**, the U.S. was sending huge **convoys** of ships across the Atlantic Ocean with supplies. The British were getting most of their food and oil from the U.S. Without those supplies, Britain had no chance of survival.

But the U.S. supply ships were in great danger. Hitler was using submarines to attack and sink them. He knew that if he could destroy Britain's lifeline, he would win the war.

The U-boats, as the German submarines were called, patrolled the sea in

German subs like this one sank many Allied supply ships during the war's early years.

In 1940, German submarines were sinking supply ships headed from the U.S. to Great Britain. The subs, which patrolled the Atlantic Ocean, got their orders via coded messages from leaders in Berlin, the capital of Germany.

deadly groups called "wolf packs." They lay just below the surface, waiting for the American ships. As the convoys drew near, the subs attacked them. They had sunk hundreds of ships since the war began.

U-boat captains took their orders directly from German commanders in Berlin. The orders were sent by radio. British radio operators could **intercept** them. But they couldn't

A tanker sinks after being hit by a torpedo from a German U-boat.

make sense of them. The coded messages looked like gibberish.

Britain's navy wasn't powerful enough to fight off the U-boats. But the British did have a secret weapon: brainpower. A team of brilliant thinkers was brought together at an old mansion codenamed Station X. They were working on a top-secret project designed to break the Germans' code. If they couldn't find a way to crack the code—and stop the wolf packs—Britain was sunk.

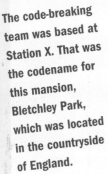

The code-breaking team was based at Station X. That was the codename for this mansion, Bletchley Park, which was located in the countryside of England.

A Mysterious Machine

The Germans thought nobody could break their code. The British were determined to prove them wrong.

The code breakers at Station X knew that German radio operators used a cipher machine called Enigma to translate all military messages into code. Cipher machines substitute each letter in a message with another letter. (See box on page 22.) But Enigma was no ordinary coding device. It was by far the most advanced one ever invented.

Enigma had a number of wheels, or **rotors**. Each rotor had the letters of the alphabet on it. The rotors could be set up in many different ways.

Pressing a letter on the keyboard would send an electrical current through the rotors. That caused one rotor to turn and a series of letter substitutions to take place. The result was that a totally different letter would light up. The operator would write that new letter down and then type in the next letter of the message.

The machine turned a plain message into a series of meaningless letters. This scrambled message would then be transmitted.

To **decipher** a message, a U-boat radio operator needed an identical Enigma machine. He also needed to know the exact rotor

Enigma looked like a simple machine. But its code was the most complex ever invented. The Germans were sure that nobody could ever crack it.

settings used by the sender. After adjusting the settings on his machine to match the sender's, the operator typed in the coded message, and the real message was quickly revealed.

British spies had captured a few early versions of the Enigma machine. But the Germans kept making adjustments to the machine, leaving British decoders in the dark.

A CODE-MAKING MACHINE

Enigma was a complex cipher machine. But simpler versions of this type of device have been around for a long time.

The most basic cipher machine is made of two circles of paper.

A larger, outer wheel shows the letters A–Z in alphabetical order around its edge.

A smaller, inner wheel has the alphabet printed on it—in random order.

To write a secret message, the sender first turns the small wheel to set the key for the code. For instance, he may line the J on the small wheel with the A on the large, alphabetical wheel.

The sender then finds the letters of his message on the outer wheel. He substitutes them with the matching letters on the inner wheel.

Unless the receiver has an identical cipher wheel, the message is just a string of nonsense letters. The receiver must also know how the wheels were set when his friend coded the message. By using the same setting, the receiver can unscramble the message.

Station X

It took people with many different skills to crack the code.

The code breakers at Station X were an odd mix. There were mathematicians and scientists. There were puzzle fanatics and chess champions. There were even some experts in reading ancient Egyptian writing. They studied intercepted messages, searching for clues.

In March 1941, spies snagged two Engima machines. They were brought back to Station X. But still, the code breakers weren't making progress fast enough to help the convoys.

U-boat radio operators used Enigma machines to decode messages from commanders on land.

All that changed on May 9. British destroyers were escorting a convoy when U-boats fired on the supply ships. A destroyer chased one of the U-boats and dropped a depth charge—a kind of bomb that explodes underwater. It was a perfect hit. The explosion pushed the U-boat to the surface. Thinking that the sub was about to sink, the crew abandoned ship. David Balme, a young officer on the destroyer *Bulldog*, volunteered to search the submarine.

Balme boarded the boat nervously, not sure if there were any German sailors still aboard. The only light came from dim blue emergency lights. With his pistol drawn, he made his way to the captain's cabin. There, he found a sealed envelope. He turned it over to his superiors. It wasn't until 30 years later that he found out what was inside that envelope.

Victory!

Another machine finally defeats Enigma.

The code breakers at Station X were overjoyed when they opened the envelope. It contained codebooks with Enigma settings and other documents. This information made it possible for them to decipher messages about U-boat positions. Now they had the information they needed to protect the convoys from the wolf packs—at least for a while.

German commanders had no idea that the British had captured the documents, so they didn't change their codes right away. Over time they did alter the Enigma system, and the code breakers had a hard time keeping up.

But soon the code breakers got another big break. A brilliant young mathematician named Alan Turing was working away in an attic

Alan Turing created a computing machine that helped the Allies win the war.

room. He believed it was possible to build a machine that could do calculations far faster than people.

Turing's machine was built, and soon it was testing thousands of possible Enigma settings every hour. By the end of the war there were 200 of the machines at Station X, helping to decode 90,000 messages a month. The Turing machine is often called the first computer. But unlike today's computers, it could solve only one problem—cracking Enigma.

The Germans never knew how the British were getting all their information. They still believed that Enigma could not be broken. They searched desperately for spies in their ranks. But their problem wasn't spies—it was a group of dedicated people working in secret at Station X. Using brains rather than bullets, these men and women fought as hard as soldiers on the front line. Their work saved many thousands of lives. And they played a huge role in the Allies' victory over Germany. 24/7

Thousands of code breakers worked around the clock at Station X. Historians estimate that their work shortened the war by at least two years.

STATION X TO THE RESCUE

In the spring of 1941, the code breakers saved a British convoy—and sank a fleet of enemy ships.

Mavis Lever was just 19 years old when she went to work at Station X. Her job was to decode messages from the Italian Navy. Italy was one of Germany's allies. And they used the Enigma machines, too.

Most of the messages Lever and her team saw were just short bits of information. But one night they decoded a long, detailed message.

A Major Attack

The Italian command was ordering a major attack on a British convoy in the Mediterranean. The message told how many Italian ships would be involved. It told where these Italian ships were. And it even said when the attack would take place.

The information was rushed to British admiral Andrew Cunningham. Cunningham's fleet was docked in Alexandria, Egypt. He knew he could attack the Italians and save the British convoy. But if he ordered his ships to sea right away, spies in Alexandria would tell the Italians.

Tricking the Spies

Cunningham announced that he was going ashore to play golf. Then, later that night, he sneaked back on board and led a surprise attack on the Italian Navy.

It was a great victory for Britain, and for Station X. As Mavis Lever said years later, "There's nothing like seeing a code broken. That is really absolutely the tops."

Cracking Enigma was a major triumph for the Allies. But no one would describe the next case as a success story.

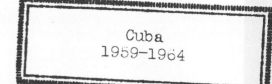

Cuba
1959–1964

A Secret Plan

An anti-American leader took over in Cuba. The CIA tried to get rid of him—in some very strange ways.

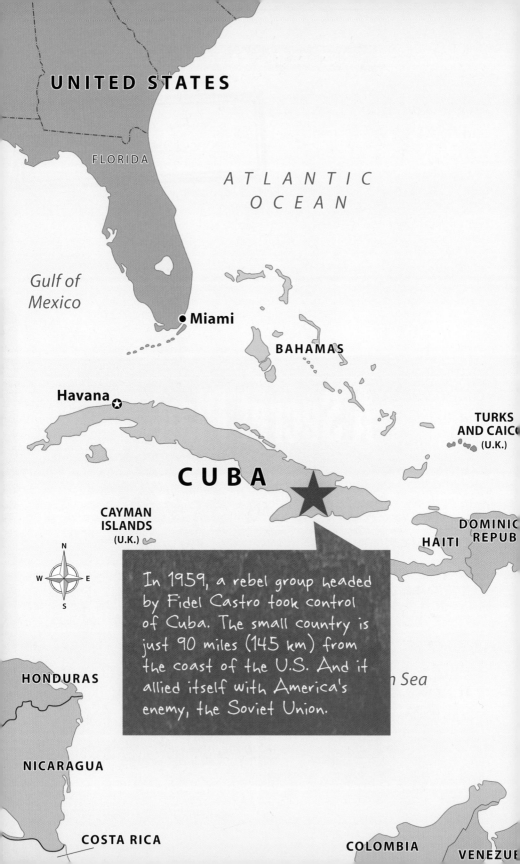

UNITED STATES

FLORIDA

ATLANTIC OCEAN

Gulf of Mexico

●Miami

BAHAMAS

Havana ✪

TURKS AND CAICO (U.K.)

CUBA

CAYMAN ISLANDS (U.K.)

DOMINIC REPUB

HAITI

N
W E
S

In 1959, a rebel group headed by Fidel Castro took control of Cuba. The small country is just 90 miles (145 km) from the coast of the U.S. And it allied itself with America's enemy, the Soviet Union.

HONDURAS

n Sea

NICARAGUA

COSTA RICA

COLOMBIA

VENEZUE

Too Close for Comfort

An anti-American government takes over in Cuba, and the U.S. gets worried.

On January 1, 1959, a revolution took place in Cuba. An army of **rebels** marched into the capital city of Havana. They overthrew the **dictator** and took control of the government.

Cuba is only 90 miles (145 km) from the coast of Florida. So leaders in the United States keep a close eye on this small country.

And after the revolution, they didn't like what they saw. The rebels were **Communists**. They believed that land and property belonged to all people—not to individuals.

The rebels took control of American-owned sugar and fruit companies. They shut down the casinos where rich Americans and gangsters liked to gamble.

What's more, the rebels became allies with the Soviet Union. At the time, the Soviet Union was the world's most powerful Communist country.

It was also America's greatest enemy.

Castro (*at the microphones*) speaks to a huge crowd shortly after seizing power.

After the revolution, Cuban leader Fidel Castro took many people's property. He also became a dictator.

Suddenly, that enemy was right at America's doorstep. What if the Soviets placed **nuclear missiles** in Cuba? A nuclear attack could come without warning.

American leaders feared that the U.S. was in danger. They decided to overthrow Cuba's Communist government. That meant getting rid of its president, Fidel Castro.

A Secret Plot

The CIA is given the task of getting rid of Fidel Castro.

Fidel Castro was probably on John F. Kennedy's mind when he became U.S. president in January 1961. One of Kennedy's first tasks was to get rid of the Cuban leader.

Kennedy knew it wouldn't be easy. And he knew it would have to be done secretly. World opinion would turn against the U.S. if word of a plot got out.

Kennedy gave the Central Intelligence Agency two choices. CIA agents could kill

Castro. Or they could destroy his reputation so he would have to step down.

At about this time, the young president met one of his favorite writers, Ian Fleming. Fleming was the creator of Bond—*James* Bond. Did Fleming have any ideas about how to **eliminate** Castro? After all, Bond always managed to eliminate *his* enemies.

Fleming jokingly suggested that the CIA find a way to get rid of Castro's beard. It was a big part of his image. If Castro lost his beard, he would look more ordinary. Soon, he would lose his power. The president laughed. It sounded like something that could only work in a James Bond book.

But that wasn't the last time the plot to kill Castro would sound like something out of a spy thriller. Many of the ideas about how to get rid of Fidel Castro could have been torn right from the pages of Ian Fleming's works.

President Kennedy believed that Castro was a major threat to U.S. security.

Mission Impossible?

CIA agents come up some strange plans to get rid of Castro.

Ian Fleming's spy, James Bond, always had the coolest gadgets. He had a watch that could shoot darts with a flick of the wrist. His pen was really a grenade. His key chain was filled with sleeping gas. Bond also had a car that could turn into a submarine. Another car had sharp blades in the hubcaps that could shred the tires of a bad guy's car.

Of course, CIA agents didn't have those kinds of gadgets. But they did dream up some Bond-like schemes for getting rid of Castro. The details of many of those operations are still secret. But information about some of them has leaked out. Here are a few of the schemes.

The CIA planned to give Castro a box of poisoned cigars. But he never received them.

► Castro loved smoking cigars, so agents planted deadly bacteria in his favorite cigars. When Castro came to a meeting at the United Nations in New York City, the poison cigars were put in a gift box for him. But he never received the gift. The CIA also had a plan to give the leader exploding cigars.

▶ The Cuban leader enjoyed scuba diving, so CIA agents designed a deadly diving suit for him. They put germs of a serious disease in the breathing device. The plan was for an insider to give the suit to Castro. It failed when the man gave Castro another suit instead.

▶ The CIA searched for a conch shell big enough to hold explosives. The idea was to paint the shell a bright color and then plant it where Castro went diving. Attracted by its size and color, he would pick it up, and the shell would explode. Like many of the plots, this one never got past the planning stages.

CIA technicians sometimes disguised deadly weapons as common objects. But the exploding seashell and poison pen were not successful designs.

▶ Agents came up with a scheme to spray a drug in the radio station where Castro broadcast his speeches. The drug would make Castro sound crazy, and Cuban citizens would demand that he step down.

▶ One plan was to use a fountain pen to inject Castro with a lethal

poison. But no agent could ever get close enough to him to do it.

The U.S. also tried secret military action. In 1961, President Kennedy backed a plan to support Cuban **exiles** who wanted to overthrow Castro. On April 17, about 1,500 exiles launched a surprise attack at Cuba's Bay of Pigs. Within two days, 90 of them had been killed. The rest had been taken prisoner. The failed mission was a major embarrassment for President Kennedy.

A Survivor

Castro considered himself indestructible. And it turned out that he was right.

A film called *638 Ways to Kill Castro* claims that there were more than 600 attempts on Castro's life. With so many enemies, how did he manage to stay alive?

For one thing, he moved around a lot between his many homes. He also used look-alikes to confuse people. His spies kept him informed about threats to his life. And bodyguards protected him around the clock.

The CIA looked for people who could get past his bodyguards. One time, agents **recruited** a former girlfriend, Marita Lorenz, to kill him with poison pills.

Lorenz hid the pills in a jar of face cream. But by the time she met with Castro, the pills had melted in the cream. By then Castro had guessed what she was up to. Knowing that she would not have the nerve to pull the trigger, he offered her his gun. "I can't do it, Fidel," she said.

In 1964, the U.S. abandoned the goal of overthrowing or eliminating Castro. Cuban exiles continued to try to kill him but never succeeded. No wonder Castro once boasted, "If surviving **assassination** attempts were an Olympic event, I would win the gold medal."

As Castro grew older, he joked about how indestructible he was. One time he was given a Galápagos turtle as a gift. These turtles can live up to 100 years. Castro returned the gift, saying, "That's the problem with pets. You get attached to them and then they die on you." 24/7

In 2006, Castro handed over his responsibilities to his brother, but kept the title of president.

The next case is about an FBI agent who turned against his country and became a Soviet spy.

Washington, D.C.
1967-1985

An American Traitor

John Walker seemed like the guy next door. But for 17 years, he was the Soviet Union's most successful spy.

Dead Drop Disaster

He made millions selling secrets to the Soviet Union. Then one day his luck ran out.

On May 19, 1985, John Anthony Walker Jr. was driving along a quiet country road outside Washington, D.C. There was a grocery bag next to him. But this was no ordinary grocery bag. Hidden inside it were 129 stolen U.S. Navy documents.

Walker was a spy working for the Soviet Union, and he was on his way to make a dead drop. A dead drop is the method a spy uses to hand off secrets without meeting his contact in person. The spy leaves the information in a container at an agreed-upon location.

For 17 years, a spy in the nation's capital sold secrets to the enemy—the Soviet Union.

On this day, Walker was using a grocery bag. It would look like trash by the side of the road. Then he would drive to a nearby location and pick up a bag left there by his contact. Inside it he would find $200,000 in cash.

Soon Walker found the dead drop spot—a pole with a NO HUNTING sign on it. He placed a 7-Up can nearby. That was his signal that he was ready to make the swap.

Then he drove to the spot where his contact was to leave the money. The Soviet agent had left a 7-Up can there to show that he, too, was ready. So Walker drove back to the first site and put the grocery bag down next to the pole.

Walker felt calm. He had done this many times before. But when he went to pick up the money, it wasn't there. Something had gone wrong. He raced back to his drop point and saw that the grocery bag was gone. He searched through the bushes and weeds, but found nothing.

Walker drove away, his mind racing. Had his contact misunderstood the instructions? Or had the FBI finally found him out?

The Soviets gave Walker detailed maps like this one to the dead drop locations.

A Spy Is Born

Could access to secret Navy codes buy Walker the things he wanted?

John Walker joined the U.S. Navy at age 18 and became a radio operator on submarines. After 12 years, the Navy promoted him. In his new job he oversaw all radio communications with submarines in the Atlantic. That meant he had access to the secret codes used for all messages to the subs.

But Walker wasn't satisfied. He wanted more money, and he knew one way he could make lots of it.

This was a time of great tension between the U.S. and the Soviet Union. Known as the **Cold War**, it lasted from the end of World War II to the late 1980s. Both superpowers had many nuclear weapons but never went to war. They did, however, spend lots of time spying on each other.

One day in 1967, Walker copied some secret codes and drove to the Soviet Embassy in Washington, D.C. There he met with an agent from the Soviet spy agency—the **KGB**. "I am interested in selling classified U.S. government documents," he told a KGB agent. "I've brought along a sample."

The KGB agent bought the codes for a

few thousand dollars. Then Walker offered to supply the agency with a steady stream of U.S. secrets. The agent agreed to pay him well, and a spy was born.

KGB agents trained Walker and gave him the equipment he would need. They taught him how to use a tiny camera to photograph secret documents. They also gave him a small device designed to read the coding machines used by the Navy. He later described that gadget as being "real James Bond."

Walker and many other spies used small cameras like this one. It could be held in one hand and took excellent photos. The camera is less than 3 inches (almost 8 cm) long.

Kiss and Tell

It was all so simple. But then Walker got too greedy.

For the next 17 years, John Walker stole more than a million secrets. His motto was KISS—which stood for "Keep It Simple, Stupid." Walker lived by that motto. His technique was simple. And it never changed. He photographed codes. Then he left the information at a dead drop site.

This information was extremely valuable to the Soviets. For one thing, it allowed them to know the exact location of America's nuclear subs. According to one KGB general, Walker gave the Soviets "the equivalent of a seat inside your Pentagon where we could read your most vital secrets."

Selling secrets made Walker rich. He owned sports cars, a plane, and a boat.

Eventually Walker retired from the Navy. But he didn't quit spying. His son, brother, and a good friend were still in the Navy. Walker recruited them to steal secrets.

To Walker, it must have seemed like the good life would go on forever. But in 1985, Walker's ex-wife turned on him. She had known about his spying, and after she and Walker argued about money, she reported

I DROP IT HERE

#4

THE TREES

YOU GO THIS WAY

Walker's Soviet handlers gave him photos like this one that showed him where to leave the stolen documents. Notice the instructions to Walker on this photo.

him to the FBI. The FBI began watching Walker and monitoring his phone calls.

On Walker's last day as a spy, FBI agents followed him down that quiet country road outside Washington, D.C.

The agents watched as Walker reached the dead drop location and left the grocery bag and the 7-Up can. After Walker drove away, they opened the grocery bag and found the stolen documents. It was just the evidence they needed to bust him. They also grabbed the 7-Up can. That's why the Soviet agent never got the signal to leave Walker the money.

Later that day, Walker checked into a nearby motel. He was anxious that things hadn't gone as planned. Why hadn't the KGB left his payment? Was it just a mix-up with his KGB contact? Or was the FBI on his trail?

At 3:30 A.M., the phone rang in Walker's motel room. A clerk at the front desk told Walker his van had been hit by another car. Walker said he would be right down.

To Walker, it sounded like the oldest trick in the book. Was the FBI outside, waiting for him? If so, he knew he should get rid of the KGB instructions he was carrying. He decided to hide them in an ice machine in the hall. With a pistol in his hand, he opened the door. The hall was empty. Relieved, Walker headed toward the ice machine.

"Stop! FBI!" Two agents in bulletproof vests were pointing their guns at him. After 17 years as the Soviets' most successful spy, Walker had finally been caught.

Since Walker's capture, he has never shown any remorse for betraying his country. He is currently serving two life sentences for his crimes. 24/7

In 1985, Walker pleaded guilty to espionage charges and was sentenced to two life terms in prison.

SPY DOWNLOAD

What's it like to be a spy? Here's more intelligence on spies past and present.

IN THIS SECTION:

- ▶ the first spies to use invisible ink;
- ▶ parents who spy on their kids;
- ▶ two real-life spies spill the beans;
- ▶ do you have what it takes to be a secret agent?

1

6th Century B.C. The Importance of Spies
Sun Tzu (*left*) was a general in ancient China. He believed that the army with the best intelligence would always win the battle. His book, *The Art of War*, is still read by military leaders today. In it he wrote: "An army without secret agents is like a man without eyes or ears."

Key Dates in the History of Spying

Every army since ancient times has spied on its enemies.

2

14th-Century Venice A Nest of Spies
Venice was a wealthy republic with many enemies. Its leaders established a group called the Council of Ten to protect Venice from plots against it. But the council became very powerful. Soon its secret police were spying on everyone in Venice.

3

1776 A Revolutionary Idea
George Washington's spies were the first to use invisible ink. It was called Jay's Sympathetic Stain. Washington called it "white ink." The writing disappeared when the ink dried. The message could only be read after it was brushed with a special solution.

1861—1865 The Civil War

One of Lincoln's first acts as president was to hire a detective named Allan Pinkerton to create a spy service. Many of Pinkerton's agents went south in disguise to gather information about the Confederate Army. One of Pinkerton's best agents was his 16-year-old son, William. Because he was so young, nobody suspected him of being a spy.

1942—1945 Navajo Code Talkers

During World War II, the Marines in the Pacific relied on a code that the Japanese could not break. It was based on the Navajo language. More than 400 Navajo men became radio operators for the Marines. These "code talkers" played a major role in all the Marines' victories in the Pacific.

1945-1991 Cold War Cameras

After World War II, the Soviet Union and the United States became nuclear superpowers. They weren't at war, but there was great tension between them. Spies were at the front lines of this so-called Cold War. Cameras and listening devices were their most important weapons. The most popular camera was the Minox C (*above*). It was tiny but it took great pictures.

1978 A Lethal Umbrella

On September 7, 1978, Bulgarian journalist Georgi Markov was walking in London. Suddenly he felt a sharp pain in his right thigh. Looking around, he saw a man with an umbrella step into a taxi. The pain in Markov's leg quickly got worse, and he died three days later. Detectives discovered that he had been killed by the man with the umbrella. The assassin had jabbed the umbrella's sharpened tip into Markov's leg and fired a poison pellet into him. The police never caught the killer.

Keeping an Eye on the Kids

He's got his eye on you—his left eye, to be exact. This cuddly spy monitors everything that happens in the room.

CHICAGO—February 27, 2006

Companies that sell spy gear report a huge growth in sales over the past ten years. One big seller is the Nanny Cam. It's a camera hidden inside a stuffed toy or other object. Parents use Nanny Cams to see how their babysitters—and kids—behave when they're not home.

Now there's a new way for parents to spy on their kids. It's called the Snoop Stick. It looks like a flash drive. Parents can plug the stick into a kid's computer and install some secret software. It takes less than a minute. Then they plug it into their own computers and spy on the kid's IMs, e-mail, and Web browsing.

If that sounds creepy, think about this. Anybody can use a Snoop Stick to spy on anybody else. Is someone watching you—right this second?

Cheats Use Spy Gear to Beat the Odds

LONDON, ENGLAND—January 15, 2007

Bit Chai Wong was on a roll at the Mint Casino. She was winning almost every hand. But her luck ran out when the staff became suspicious. They thought she might have some tricks up her sleeve. And they were right.

Wong and two partners were using high-tech spy gear to cheat at cards. One wore a tiny video camera up his sleeve. Images of his cards were beamed to a van outside. The man in the van then spoke to Wong, who was wearing a tiny earpiece. He told her what the other player's cards were. That allowed her to play one winning hand after another.

The gang has pulled the same scam at casinos all over London. They have pocketed an estimated $500,000. Wong and her partners pleaded guilty and were sentenced to nine months in prison.

A spy cam made it possible for cheater Bit Chai Wong to win big at poker.

HELP WANTED:
Secret Agents

Interested in the world of espionage? Here's more information about the field.

Q&A: JONNA MENDEZ

Jonna Mendez is the former chief of disguise for the CIA.

24/7: How did you become a spy?

JONNA MENDEZ: I was living in Europe and working at an American bank. One of the customers became my first husband. I found out two days before the wedding that he worked for the CIA. Through him, I got a job as a secretary for the CIA. But I wanted to do more. I went to work in the Office of Technical Service. We made all the gadgets. If an agent needed something to do his operation, we'd make it.

24/7: What kind of gadgets did you make?

MENDEZ: I became an expert in small cameras. Miniature cameras can be hidden in a pen, a button, a lighter, or a lipstick. We gave these cameras to our foreign agents so they could steal the secrets in their offices. If someone walked in and they were sitting at their desk holding a "pen," it didn't look suspicious.

24/7: How did you go from gadgets to disguises?

MENDEZ: I wanted to work in India, and the only position there was in the disguise division. I went through training to learn all about disguise. Eventually, I became deputy chief and then chief of disguise. I spent a lot of time coming up with new disguise systems. As chief, I had people who worked for me stationed around the world. I traveled a lot to train foreign agents. I loved meeting new people and seeing new countries. I liked the adventure. I liked that I was helping my country.

24/7: What was the hardest part of your job?

MENDEZ: You could never tell anybody what you were doing. My best friend thought I had a boring government job. After I retired, she found out I worked for the CIA. She felt I wasn't as open as a best friend ought to be. I lost a good friend.

24/7: What was a typical day like?

MENDEZ: Going to the office was like walking into a wind tunnel. You never knew what was coming at you. You would read cables from all around the world. You found out where you were going to send people, where somebody needed help, where materials needed to be delivered. There was rarely a dull moment.

24/7: What advice can you give young people interested in this career?

MENDEZ: If you'd like to help your country, this is a great way to do it. These days there are lots of opportunities to explore the world of spying. The International Spy Museum is a great way to find out about spying and gadgets. The CIA has a site for kids. There are even a lot of spy camps for kids.

THE STATS

MONEY: Starting salary is around $40,000 a year.

THE NUMBERS: The CIA won't disclose how many people it employs. It receives more than 10,000 applications each month.

REQUIREMENTS: The CIA looks for smart and trustworthy people with these qualifications:
▶ a college degree with a minimum GPA of 3.0;
▶ a taste for travel and adventure;
▶ in good physical shape;
▶ a second language is a must for those who want to work overseas.

HELP WANTED:
Secret Agents

Q&A: CHASE BRANDON

Chase Brandon is a
former CIA officer.

24/7: How did you get interested in espionage?

CHASE BRANDON: I watched James Bond movies and
thought that would be a neat job. Then in junior year
of college, a CIA recruiter met with me. I was the type
of person the agency was looking for. I was a pilot, a
parachutist, a hunter, and a scuba diver. I also knew
Spanish and had good grades.

24/7: What was training like?

BRANDON: We had espionage training where you learn
disguise, secret writing, and surveillance. You also learn
to enter buildings secretly and to take photos without
anyone knowing. Then came paramilitary training—
jumping out of planes, escape and evasion, high-speed
driving, **counterterrorism** tactics, weapons, and
martial arts.

24/7: What was your role as a spy?

BRANDON: I was more of a spy master than a spy, meaning I
would find agents to bring me the information rather than
me trying to get information myself. I had to find the moles

and **double agents**. This was during the Cold War. We were in a war of ideas with the Soviet Union. What was at stake was the possibility of nuclear war if it got out of hand.

24/7: Did your agents use gadgets?

BRANDON: Gadgets and gizmos were the wrenches, screwdrivers, and pliers of a spy's toolbox. They included miniature cameras, concealment devices, codes, transmitters, little radios, disguises, and lock picks. All the things you've seen in the Bond movies. I trained my agents to use all of these gadgets.

24/7: What's the hardest part of being a spy?

BRANDON: Being removed from family and friends for a long time is hard. It's also hard to know that some of your colleagues may be injured or killed. Plus, some of the agents you recruit are not people you like. But you have to act like they're your friends because they have access to really important information. Also, if you're disrupting terrorists or drug traffickers, they will want to harm you. And your family could be in danger as well.

24/7: What does it take to be a CIA officer?

BRANDON: For us, the most important qualities are integrity, honesty, **patriotism**, intellectual curiosity, and a sense of adventure. Espionage is a criminal capital offense in every country—so you need to understand what you're doing. You're really lying and stealing for the U.S. government. You need a profound sense of patriotism and good citizenship. You have to believe our nation is worth defending. When we interview job candidates, we pull every layer of your onion back because we want to know everything about who you are as a person.

BRANDON IS A CONSULTANT ON TV SHOWS SUCH AS *24* AND MOVIES SUCH AS *MISSION IMPOSSIBLE III*.

DO YOU HAVE WHAT IT TAKES?

Take this totally unscientific quiz to see if espionage might be a good career for you.

 1 Can you keep a secret?

a) My friends tell me everything because they know I'll never say a word.

b) Sometimes. But when you hear something really juicy, it's hard to keep it to yourself.

c) Are you kidding? I'm a total blabbermouth.

2 Do you enjoy pretending to be somebody else?

a) I've been in lots of school plays. I love getting into costume and playing a character.

b) I do pretty good impressions of my friends, but that's about it.

c) Even if I'm a zombie on Halloween, everyone knows it's me.

3 Do you get scared easily?

a) No way. It takes a lot to frighten me.

b) I love roller coasters. But I cover my eyes during scary scenes in the movies.

c) What can I say? I'm scared of mice.

4 Do you consider yourself patriotic?

a) Very much so. I believe everyone should try to serve his or her country in some way.

b) I'm proud of my country, but it's not something I think about a lot.

c) I think of myself as a citizen of the world.

YOUR SCORE

Give yourself 3 points for every "**a**" you chose. Give yourself 2 points for every "**b**" you chose. Give yourself 1 point for every "**c**" you chose.

If you got **10–12 points**, you probably have the right stuff to become a spy. If you got **7–9 points**, you might be a good intelligence analyst. If you got **4–6 points**, you might want to look at another career!

HOW TO GET STARTED ... NOW!

GET AN EDUCATION

▶ Take a wide variety of courses, including history. Make sure you take computer science courses. Learn at least one foreign language.

▶ Read the newspapers and magazines. Stay informed about world affairs.

▶ Read anything you can find about spies. Check out books on espionage from the library. Learn about how the intelligence community works. Read spy novels, too, for fun. See the books and Web sites in the Resources section on pages 56–58.

▶ Graduate from high school! You'll need to go to college to work in espionage.

▶ Join the drama club. Try out for the school play.

It's never too early to start working toward your goals.

GET INVOLVED

▶ Call the cops. Many police departments have programs for teen volunteers. You can get to know police work from the inside. Police work and espionage are closely related.

▶ Volunteer for community service programs.

LEARN ABOUT OTHER JOBS IN THE FIELD!

There are other jobs that relate to intelligence work. They are:

Private detective
Home security specialist
Communications technician
Soldier
Translator
Computer programmer

Resources

Looking for more information about spies? Here are some resources you don't want to miss!

PROFESSIONAL ORGANIZATIONS

Central Intelligence Agency (CIA)
www.cia.gov
Office of Public Affairs
Washington, DC 20505
PHONE: 703-482-0623
FAX: 703-482-1739

The CIA was created in 1947 when President Harry Truman signed the National Security Act. The organization works to collect information that will help keep the United States safe. It also engages in research and development of high-level technology for gathering intelligence.

Federal Bureau of Investigation (FBI)
www.fbi.gov
J. Edgar Hoover Building
935 Pennsylvania Avenue, NW
Washington, DC 20535
PHONE: 202-324-3000

The FBI works to protect and defend the United States from terrorism and foreign threats. It also upholds the criminal laws of the United States and provides leadership for federal, state, and local law enforcement.

National Security Agency/Central Security Service (NSA/CSS)
www.nsa.gov
9800 Savage Road, Suite 6248
Fort George G. Meade, MD 20755
PHONE: 301-688-6524

The NSA/CSS is the U.S. Cryptologic agency. It coordinates and directs highly specialized activities to protect U.S. government information. It is also a center for foreign language analysis and research.

U.S. Department of State
www.state.gov
2201 C Street, NW
Washington, DC 20520
PHONE: 202-647-4000

The mission of the U.S. State Department is to create a more secure, democratic, and prosperous world for people in the United States and the international community. The people at the State Department use diplomacy, negotiation, and intelligence to work with other countries.

WEB SITES

Bletchley Park
www.bletchleypark.org.uk
Visit this site to learn more about World War II's Station X.

CIA Careers
www.cia.gov/careers/index.html
This site offers information about working for the CIA, including a fun personality quiz.

CIA Museum
www.cia.gov/cia/information/ artifacts/index.htm
Visit this site to take an online look at some great spy gadgets.

Crime Library
www.crimelibrary.com/terrorists_ spies/spies/index.html
This section of the crime library has true stories about terrorists, spies, and assassins.

FBI Kids' Page
www.fbi.gov/fbikids.htm
You can play games and read tips and stories to learn more about the FBI.

International Spy Museum
www.spymuseum.org/index.asp
This musem offeres information about both human and animal spies throughout history.

National Cryptologic Museum
www.nsa.gov/museum/
Check out these exhibits to learn more about ciphering throughout history.

Spy Letters of the American Revolution
www.si.umich.edu/spies/
This site has a collection of letters and other information about spies during the American Revolution.

U.S. Department of State Careers
www.state.gov/careers
This site provides information about what positions are available at the State Department and how to apply for them.

PROFESSIONAL BOOKS

Abraham, Philip. *The CIA* (Top Secret). Danbury, Conn.: Children's Press, 2003.

Bursztynski, Sue. *This Book Is Bugged* (It's True!). Toronto: Annick Press, 2007.

Coleman, Janet Wyman, and the International Spy Museum. *Secrets, Lies, Gizmos, and Spies: A History of Spies and Espionage.* New York: Abrams Books for Young Readers, 2006.

Dowswell, Paul, and Fergus Fleming. *True Spy Stories.* Minneapolis: Tandem Library, 2004.

Hindley, Judy, and Lesley Sims, eds. *The Usborne Spies Guidebook.* London: Usborne Books, 2000.

January, Brendan. *The CIA* (Watts Library). Danbury, Conn.: Watts Library, 2002.

Keeley, Jennifer. *The Cold War: Espionage* (American War Library). San Diego: Lucent Books, 2002.

Owen, David. *Spies: The Undercover World of Secrets, Gadgets, and Lies.* New York: Firefly Books, 2004.

Portalupi, Laura. *Spies! Real People, Real Stories.* Bloomington, Minn.: Red Brick Learning, 2005.

Ramaprian, Sheila. *The FBI* (Top Secret). Danbury, Conn.: Children's Press, 2003.

Sakany, Lois. *Women Civil War Spies of the Union.* New York: Rosen Publishing, 2003.

Townsend, John. *Spies* (True Crime). Austin: Raintree, 2005.

Wiese, Jim. *The Spy's Guide to Scouting and Reconnaissance.* New York: Scholastic, 2003.

Yancey, Diane. *Spies* (History Makers). San Diego: Lucent Books, 2001.

A

agents (AY-juhnts) *noun* people who collect information and perform other secret tasks on behalf of an intelligence service like the CIA

Allied (AL-eyes) *adjective* describing the forces that were opposed to Germany and Japan during World War II

ally (AL-eye) *noun* a person or group that is on your side

assassination (uh-SAH-suh-nay-shun) *noun* the murder of a government leader by sudden or secret attack

B

bug (buhg) *noun* a hidden electronic listening device

C

CIA (see-eye-AY) *noun* an agency of the U.S. government that deals with foreign intelligence (the secrets and knowledge of other countries) and counterintelligence (misleading spies from other countries). It stands for *Central Intelligence Agency*.

cipher (SYE-fur) *noun* a kind of code in which letters and numbers are replaced with other letters and numbers

code (kode) *noun* a system used to disguise a message by changing words into something else. Letters, words, or phrases are replaced by other letters, words, phrases, or even symbols.

Cold War (kold war) *noun* the period after World War II when Communist countries, such as the Soviet Union, and noncommunist countries, such as the United States, were competing against one another

Communists (KOM-yoo-nists) *noun* people who believe in communism, a system that says all property is owned by the government

convoys (KON-voyz) *noun* ships, or other vehicles, traveling in groups

counterterrorism (kown-tur-TAIR-ur-izm) *noun* organized activity to fight terrorism; terrorism is a system of violence used to frighten people, usually for political reasons.

D

dead drops (ded drops) *noun* acts of hiding items in everyday objects and leaving them someplace where other people can pick them up later

Dictionary

decipher (dee-SYE-fur) *verb* to figure out the meaning of something

dictator (DIK-tay-tur) *noun* a ruler who has complete control over a country; dictators do not have to answer to anyone and can treat their people any way they want

double agents (DUH-bul AY-jents) *noun* agents who appear to be working for one side but are really working for the other

E

eliminate (ih-LIM-uh-nayte) *verb* to destroy or get rid of something

espionage (ESS-pee-uh-nahzh) *noun* the act of using spies to gain information about the plans and activities of other groups, armies, or countries

exiles (EG-zilez) *noun* people who are forced to leave their country and live elsewhere

F

FBI (eff-bee-EYE) *noun* a U.S. government agency that fights terrorism and organized crime. It stands for the *Federal Bureau of Investigation*.

H

handler (HAN-dlur) *noun* a spy's boss

I

informant (in-FOR-muhnt) *noun* a person who supplies agents and other officials with secret information

intelligence (in-TEL-uh-juhnss) *noun* information about an enemy's plans or activities

intercept (in-tur-SEPT) *verb* to stop or seize something before it can reach its intended destination

in the wind *adjective* used to describe a target who escapes

K

KGB (kay-jee-BEE) *noun* a spy agency for the Soviet Union. It is short for *Komitet gosudarstvennoi bezopasnosti*.

M

missions (MIH-shunz) *noun* special jobs or tasks

mole (mohl) *noun* a spy who works within the enemy's spy agency

N

nuclear missiles (NOO-klee-ur MISS-uhlz) *noun* weapons that are made from nuclear reactions and can cause incredible damage

P

patriotism (PAY-tree-ooh-tih-zim) *noun* love and devotion toward your country

R

rabbit (RAB-it) *noun* the target of a surveillance operation

rebels (REH-buhlz) *noun* people who disobey a group or government and act against it

recruited (reh-KROOT-ed) *verb* hired or convinced someone to join a group

rotors (RO-turz) *noun* wheels with numbers on them

S

sleeper (SLEE-puhr) *noun* an agent who isn't active and is living as a normal citizen in another country

Soviet Union (SO-vee-uht YOON-yuhn) *noun* the former government of present-day Russia and surrounding countries

spy (spye) *noun* a person who tries to get or send information secretly

surveillance (sur-VAY-luhnss) *noun* the act of keeping a close watch or listening in on someone. It is often done in secret.

T

transmitted (TRANZ-mit-ed) *verb* sent from one person or place to another

Index

638 Ways to Kill Castro (film), 34

Author's Note

GO TO THE SOURCE To write a book about spies, I went directly to the experts on spying. First, I called the CIA. They came up with many of the gadgets that you've read about in this book.

Chase Brandon, a former spy himself, was very helpful. I visited him at CIA headquarters just outside of Washington, D.C. Although CIA security took my tape recorder and camera, I got a personal look at the devices on display in the CIA museum. Seeing those gadgets for myself really helped me understand how they work. Brandon showed me films of the robotic catfish and dragonflies designed to listen in. He also shared with me a lot of detailed information about CIA spy gadgets and his own history.

By calling the CIA, I also met Jonna Mendez, the former chief of disguise, who talks about her career in spying in this book.

If you're researching a project, try to go directly to the source. Organizations and businesses all have public relations offices that are ready to help. If you are polite and can clearly explain what you're writing about, people will often give you the information you want.

READ AND RESEARCH This book took a lot of research. I read many books on spies and the history of spying. I visited the International Spy Museum and researched gadgets online. When you do your own big projects, try to read as much as possible about your topic. Check out books from the library and search the Internet for information on your subject. The more you dig for information, the more interesting facts you will find. And the more unique facts you find, the more original your work will be.

ACKNOWLEDGMENTS

I would like to thank Chase Brandon and Jonna Mendez for being so generous with their time and sharing their personal knowledge on spying and top secret devices.

CONTENT ADVISER: Steven Aftergood, Director of the Project on Government Secrecy, Federation of American Scientists